the indoor
how-to book of
    oats, peas, beans,
    and other
    pretty plants

Also by HAZEL PERPER

The Avocado Pit Grower's
Indoor How-To Book

The Citrus Seed Grower's
Indoor How-To Book

With illustrations by Edith Kramer

the indoor how-to book of oats, peas, beans, and other pretty plants

by HAZEL PERPER

A William Cole Book

The Viking Press | New York

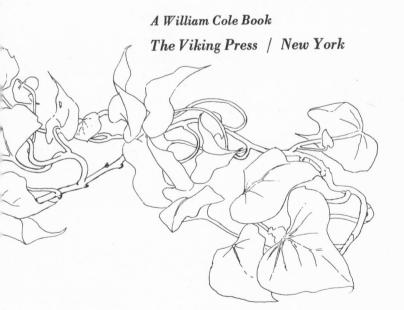

For Robbie, with love

A William Cole Book

First published in 1975 by The Viking Press, Inc.
625 Madison Avenue, New York, N.Y. 10022

Published simultaneously in Canada by
The Macmillan Company of Canada Limited

Library of Congress Cataloging in Publication Data

Perper, Hazel.
  The indoor how-to book of oats, peas, beans, and
other pretty plants.

  "A William Cole book."
  1. House plants. I. Title.
SB419.P37   635.9′65   74–31441
ISBN 0–670–39816–0

Printed in U.S.A.

contents

✥ PREFACE ✥

There was once a time when, for their parlors, the indoor gardeners of middle America favored the cultivation of rubber plants. They also liked aspidistras, and Irish ivy, and fuchsias, and begonias, and tiny palms, and mosses grown in glass cases. Then, because fashions move in cycles, styles in house plants changed. The era of the rubber plant gave way to days of African violets, and aerial orchids, and ferns, and bromeliads, and avocado trees, and cactuses, and citrus trees, and home-grown herbs and mushrooms. . . . And as indoor gardeners demanded more and more varieties of house plants to enhance their parlors, the traditions of horticulture were kept well and truly green.

In the meantime, however, we've come into an age of specialization. And while the outside world has become generally smaller, so have our homes, parlors, and living rooms. Today in every available indoor nook, corner, cranny, and crevice lush and lovely greenery can be seen under lively cultivation. What's more, though that foliage may be mostly contained in terra-cotta pots and redwood tubs, it may also be housed in bronze bowls, wicker baskets, sea shells, antique Wedgewood egg cups, fish bowls, Bohemian glass goblets, and so on and on.

Therefore, in the interests of perhaps filling in a plant-less gap or two, I suggest the cultivation of a timeless plant or two. Consider: fresh cereal grasses started from seed; the generous graceful leaves of elephant's-ears grown from taro tubers; the lovely manners of beautiful sweet potato vines started from their tubers; the sweetly scented towering blades of ginger grass rising from a gnarled root; the pastel colors and light perfumes of bean blossoms developed from a single dried bean seed; the languid drapery of pineapple leaves attached to a crown once cut from a fresh fruit. And all these can be quickly germinated to produce full green leafage cultivated at home . . . or on an office desk or factory workbench.

Times have indeed changed. But slowly enough for us to realize that to cherish the forests we have to go into them to find out how to preserve the differences and similarities between the growth and development of every individual tree, plant, blossom, seed, grass, and living creature. Herewith some updated ways and means.

1
Oats and wheat and other grasses

Oats, wheat, rye, millet, alfalfa, clover, timothy hay, and lawn grass can be cultivated indoors in a pot, bowl, shallow boat-shaped dish, or in a big pot as ground cover for a great tree. And though these grasses yield small plants they are most charming when allowed to grow tall, tangled, and left uncut.

Unlike a good-sized indoor tree, grass grown indoors will enjoy a much shorter life span. Yet there is a special appeal about green grasses germinated indoors in the depths of winter. Perhaps the sight of slender blades of oats or millet recently sown triggers racial memories of the era during which we first took to agriculture, when the emergence of tender fresh growth affirmed our control over new sources of new foods. Or perhaps the hope and expectation of a lifting panicle of rye evokes the image of an earth goddess ready and willing to transmute cereal grasses magically into spiritous liquors. My source of pleasure is simpler and more immediate.

Once I had a visit from a small person who had come to see my big avocado tree. Thriving in a large tub, the tree loomed overhead but seemed to hold no interest for her. Perhaps it stood too high, perhaps it was all too common a sight for my young friend. In any case, she kept her sights low. But her head, clearing the top of the tub

A dish of oats and lawn grass

by mere inches, brought her into a close-up view of a recently sown crop of lawn grass now growing at the base of the tree. For a moment or two she gravely studied the low lush greenery and then put out her hand, reached in, ruffled the blades of grass, and smiled. Her gesture was so like the one adults indulge in when they reach down to touch the soft fine hair on a child's head that there and then I resolved always to keep a head of grass growing somewhere in the house. And I do.

Cereal grains and grasses are among the world's oldest plants. And at the risk of sounding like a textbook straight out of my childhood, it must be added that the history of the cereal grains, wheat, for example, is so closely tied to the development of man from hunter to agriculturist that it is practically impossible to separate the two. Moreover, it must also be added that at this moment wheat breeders

10

and plant physiologists everywhere are working to improve the quality and productivity of that most nutritious grain. Many of these workers are involved with a species of wheat called einkorn which has but a single grain and is botanically classified as *Trititicum monococcum*. Said to be the most primitive wheat, einkorn has been found carbonized and impressed in the ancient soils of cultures dating back to the Neolithic. Einkorn is still highly valued because it readily hybridizes with other wheat species, grows well in poor soils, and is a general all-round tough survivor.

Botanical information on cereals and the simple grasses is so staggeringly complex and complete that it would be foolish to try even to skim it here. Suffice it to say that for our needs the seeds we want must not be damaged. If the husks have been removed by commercial processing such seeds will not germinate. (The protective husk, enveloping the seed, firmly secures the plant's nucleus and its needed nutrients.) It must be noted also that seeds will not germinate when they have passed their cycle of maturity. Older seeds may be fine for cooking and eating, but they are not so hot for sowing and reaping.

Indoor plantings of whole, unhusked cereal grains will invariably produce young plants. The chances are slim, however, that these plants will flower or fruit. True, I've grown a number of crops of indoor oats and wheat that were sown in the spring, and which in summer began to develop minuscule heads of grain. Sad to say, my heads of grain remained immature and fell away long before fall.

☙ SOURCES

Ideally, the best place to buy fertile cereal grains —or grass seed—is an old-fashioned feed-and-grain store. And if such a store is accessible, one should get into it and make some small purchases. Another source for buying whole-grain cereals is those shops that specialize in so-called "organic" foods. There one may find supplies of natural grains marked "guaranteed absolutely organic." In my experience such cereal grains begin vigorous sprouting twenty-four to thirty-six hours after planting. There are many other cereal grains to be found in these shops, and they are all worth experimenting with.

Seeds are usually packaged in small bags, and at reasonable enough prices. (Incidentally, grain sprouts, twelve to twenty-four hours above ground, are very good eaten raw on the spot, or chopped and added to a green salad.)

Lawn grasses come in many varieties and will grow indoors at any time of the year. They may be purchased at garden-supply stores. The trick is to latch onto a small quantity. Or try to scrounge some lawn-grass seeds from a country cousin or a suburbanite.

And whatever grasses you decide to cultivate, each will reveal its own shape, size, and style of development—and therein lies much of the fun.

✿ PLANTING

MATERIALS NEEDED:

An eight-inch terra-cotta pot with good drainage holes well-crocked

Soil (loamy mixture is preferred)

Crocking materials

Dish to go under pot to catch water overflow

Plant food

(See Chapter 8 for details about planting practices)

Grass and cereal seeds are usually quite small. A good rule of thumb to follow when planting them is to place the seed no deeper than a quarter of an inch underground. Spaces between seeds need be no more than half an inch, and no less than one quarter inch. Grasses want good drainage, so crock your pot generously. For a loamy soil use "general potting mixture," which is sold commercially under that label. Or add a cup of coarse sand—sterilized—to "humus-enriched soil," also sold commercially under that descriptive label. Fill the pot to within an inch of its top with the soil mixture. Apply water so the soil is moist throughout, but no wetter than that. Now plant the seeds. Put a dish under the pot and place both pot and dish in a shaded spot. During the time seeds are germinating underground, apply water in gentle dribbles to prevent the seeds from being flushed to the surface of the soil when watered. Seeds should sprout within thirty-six hours, give or take a few hours. As soon as the sprouts emerge, move the pot into shaded sunlight, or at least ten inches from two 100-watt bulbs. Once the blades begin to uncurl into stalks of grass, mist-spray them with tepid water and continue to do so every other day thereafter . . . especially important when temperatures rise above 75° F. As the grass rises higher, you may well wonder at the mechanism that the plant employs to pump up exact quantities of water to provide each blade's topmost tip with its own crystal-clear droplet. After three or four days of this self-watering performance, the mechanism shuts off, and now it is time to move the planted pot into full sunlight or artificial light. Be sure to guard against extremes of heat and cold. More than two hours in hot summer sunlight will scorch tender grasses, and icy blasts of wind will kill them.

Be sure as well to apply only enough water to keep the soil damp. Three weeks after the emergence of the blades, leave the plant unwatered for at least twenty-four hours. Then give a stingy supply of plant food (if you're using tablets and the packaged recipe calls for two tablets, give one) and apply enough water to moisten soil. Repeat these day-long droughts once a week.

Sometimes it is desirable to give a stand of grasses a support of sorts, though this is no more than a nicety. When grasses grow taller than expected, a fence helps keep the blades from flopping over the edges of the pot. I make a six-inch-high circular fence with thin wooden sticks, no heavier than a toothpick, which I push into the earth around the inside edge of the pot. I then connect the little posts with a lacing of thread or some fine string which does the job quite nicely.

In the course of further growing events, it is possible that some of your grasses may flower. It does not happen often, and if it does occur it may well pass unnoticed because the flowers are small and fade quickly. Keep in mind, however, that a subsequent development of heads of grain is still doubtful, even when blossoms are seen.

Try planting whatever other grasses come to hand— timothy, clover, and so on. My greatest accomplishment to date has been the continued development of a dandelion plant that I uprooted in the country, brought home, and planted in an eight-inch pot. To my delight a brilliant yellow flower soon came into full blossom, then slowly turned to a white, downy ball of fine fluff. I gathered up the flighty seeds as they blew free and planted them, but nothing came of that second trial run.

However, when one variety of grass after another is sown in a pattern of successive circles around a flourishing ginger or blossoming bean plant, the potted foliage can become a green centerpiece so lush and handsome it is fit for holiday table settings.

2 🪻 Beans and peas 🪻

       Cultivated as food for humans and domestic animals alike, the international yearly crop of dried beans and peas today is reckoned in the billions of tons. And one dried red kidney bean, planted indoors at any time, is almost certain to take root and become a pretty plant that will produce blossoms and go on to yield a small but tasty crop of fresh green beans.

Beans and peas are classified—confusingly—under one family name, *Leguminosae*. Now the term legume, usually pluralized, is applied in Europe and elsewhere to any vegetable offered as food. In this country the word legume is seldom heard at our dinner tables or supermarkets, yet the words beans and peas seem to be used interchangeably on packages of dried legumes. However, we know the difference between fresh green beans and sweet peas when they are served as cooked vegetables. And it might be added that while beans and peas are sometimes cultivated for their pods—usually as cattle fodder—they are mostly cultivated for their nutritious edible seeds that, after being removed from their generally inedible pods, are eaten by people everywhere.

In the supermarket, where I have admired large displays of packaged dried beans, I have often goggled at the differently sized, shaped, colored, and named varieties at hand.

A frieze of pinto-bean sprouts

After one recent goggle, I turned to bookish sources and was disconcerted to read that six hundred genera and twelve thousand species of beans and peas have been identified, running a gamut from the gorgeously flowered royal poinciana tree of the tropics (heading the great *Leguminosae* family) to the *Phaseolus* genus which includes such familiar species as the kidney bean, the lima bean, and the dark-green mung bean. Though the mung bean is said to be popular in the Far East, boiled in tea and served as a kind of mush, it is highly valued today in this country, and elsewhere in the world, for its delectable crisp sprouts, which anyone can germinate indoors.

BEAN SPROUTS

Not only are bean sprouts delicious and high in protein and vitamin B_1, they can also be about as fresh a vegetable as one can hope to find anywhere so close at hand. Dried mung beans are small and yellowish-green to dark-green, or even black. They are quite inexpensive, and available in many supermarkets or in shops that specialize in gourmet or so-called "organic" foods. And because the sprouts are so popular in Chinese cooking, they can be bought in markets that sell Oriental food. According to information gathered in a Chinese vegetable shop, one tablespoon of dried mung beans will provide a portion of sprouts for one person.

Sprouting is simplicity itself. What is needed are the whole beans and a wide, flat container to provide the beans with enough moisture to keep them damp while they germinate. A flat-bottomed colander placed in a shallow pan containing a constant one half inch of water will do the

16

trick. Or you may cover the bottom of a glass pie plate with two or three thicknesses of paper toweling or cheesecloth. (Rinse the cloth thoroughly before using it.)

Now, in a single flat layer, scatter the desired amount of beans over the bottom of your chosen vessel. Do not pile the beans on top of one another; spread them out flat so each bean has its own space. Then pour in enough water to cover the beans, and no more. Set the dish aside in a cool, dark place. After about six hours gently flush the beans with fresh tepid water until they are well rinsed. Leave enough water to cover beans, and again set dish aside in a cool, dark place. This rinsing and flushing procedure may be repeated every six hours, or as infrequently as two or three times a day. Just make sure that beans are kept constantly moist. Within another twenty-four hours the hulls may begin to split, and tiny sprouts will begin to emerge from the white flesh. After sixty to seventy-two hours the crisp tendrils (which should continue to be rinsed regularly and replenished with fresh water) will have grown longer, and will be ready for harvesting. When picking the sprouts, do not remove the hulls, which are rich in nourishment and flavor and can be enjoyed along with the crunchy sprouts. There is no rule about when to harvest bean sprouts; they can be allowed to grow quite long. Just don't wait so long that the beans go bad—which they will do if neglected or left to languish in a drought.

Dried soybeans, white navy beans, and small beans of other varieties can also be sprouted in a similar fashion. Remember that the larger the bean the stronger the flavor of its sprouts.

Navy-bean sprouts in various stages of breaking loose

17

PLANTING BEANS AND PEAS

Do not hesitate to plant whatever dried beans come to hand—there's a great big field to choose from. At the same time it is a good idea to avoid planting dried beans that have been packaged or stored on a shelf for a long time; such beans may have lost their fertility. (There's no test for this kind of staleness. But shops that sell lots of dried beans are likely to have freshly packed assortments on hand.)

As an alternative, consider buying fresh beans or peas and leaving them around to dry out thoroughly in their pods. I've had great good luck with fresh pinto beans bought in their pods in a Spanish bodega. I left the handsome pods in the sunlight until the skins were crackling dry. Then I shelled the lot, planted them, and grew a good number of pretty plants that gave me a nice crop of fresh beans.

SOURCES

At all times of the year, huge quantities of dried beans are available in local supermarkets, bodegas, and "organic"-food stores. While it seems unnecessary to mention that prices on everything have soared, it is pleasant to note that a package of dried kidney beans, for instance, still costs as little as fifty cents. What's more, that package is likely to contain upwards of five hundred dried beans, which is a very good buy for an indoor gardener. (Besides, leftover beans can be converted to a tasty chili.)

Hard-shelled dried beans tend to grow tougher, longer-lasting plants than do the soft-shelled varieties. It is easy to tell the difference between hard-shelled and soft-shelled beans. A soft-shelled bean is usually dimpled, as if its inner flesh had fallen in or shrunk in a number of places, leaving the coat a shade loose. Hard-shelled beans remain smooth, plump, and fit their shells nicely through all commercial handling.

18

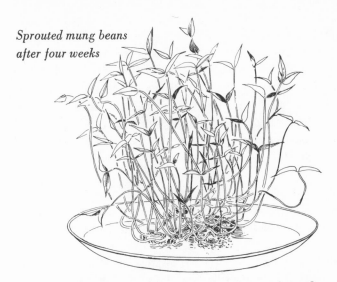

Sprouted mung beans after four weeks

Indoor bean plants may sprout after two or three days in the pot—or they may take up to ten days—and they last through a two- to three-month season of growth. After blossoming, in such colors as pastel pink, blue, or white, the plant will produce a crop of small, tender beans. Peas and beans develop either as upright bushes or as climbing vines. The size of the plant is proportionate to the size of the seed: bigger seeds yield bigger plants.

POTTING

MATERIALS NEEDED:

Whole beans or peas

Soil (general potting mixture mixed with coarse sand, both sterilized)

Terra-cotta pots, in sizes ranging from six to twelve inches

Crocking materials

Dish to go under pot to catch water overflow

Plant food

Bean poles, depending on how your plant develops

𝒮❧ℰ𝒮 *Seeds into Pot*

Cover the bottom of the pot with crocking materials at least two inches deep. Fill the crocked pot to within one inch of the top with a mixture of general potting soil, to which has been added one cupful of sterilized coarse sand. Water-soak the soil. Plant the beans to a depth of three-quarters of an inch, allowing one inch between each bean. Because only three or four beans will fit into a six-inch pot, I recommend larger pots for any beans of kidney-bean size or larger. Place the pot in direct sunlight or artificial light. When the first shoots rise into view, remove the pot to shaded light until plants are at least three inches high. Then bring pot back into direct light and leave it there. If sunlight is in short supply, three or four hours of artificial light shed by two 100-watt bulbs will do nicely when given twice daily. Don't allow the plant to get so close to the light as to scorch the tender young leaves.

Should one bean grow taller and sturdier than any of its companions, transplant the weaklings—or simply abandon them—thus leaving the hearty plant its own domain where it can flourish expansively. Beans like well-drained soil and warmth. Use only tepid water and apply it sparingly so that the bottom of the pot is not constantly wet. Once a week, allow the soil to dry out, but avoid parching for more than two days. Bean plants left in dry air for more than two days without watering—especially in winter—will soon languish.

Initial shoots emerge anywhere from four days to three weeks after planting. When greenery is established, mist-spray it once a week. Supply plant food every four weeks after the first stems and leaves are in the air. Repeat plant food at same intervals thereafter.

Once the first vulnerable shoots are placed in the sun, they reach out for the light as if fearful that that source of life might wander from its orbit unless closely watched. Therefore, from time to time, compensate for their motility

20

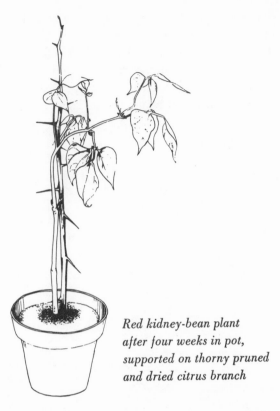

Red kidney-bean plant
after four weeks in pot,
supported on thorny pruned
and dried citrus branch

by turning the pots around so that all sides get light. And note that each time the pot is repositioned, the plant immediately sets about the business of turning around to again face the sun head-on. This is a very impressive demonstration of bean power* and it happens so rapidly you can actually watch the plant move.

* Legend has it that once a full load of dried beans was stowed for shipment in the hold of a large steel cargo vessel. Soon after setting sail, the ship sprang a slow leak. Quietly the beans began to absorb water, and as they did they started to swell and swell and swell. There then came a day when the swollen beans split the ship in two. And as the vessel sank from sight, the officers and crew, standing off in lifeboats, watched helplessly.

Within a few weeks your plant may put forth a tendril that seems determined to become a vine. The time has come to consider a bean pole. As a long-time collector of twigs and dried branches, I always have a skinny piece of wood around to serve as a bean pole. If you don't have a twig or stake, use a thin dowel about six to eight inches high and gently place it in the center of the pot. Gently tie your plant to the small stick.

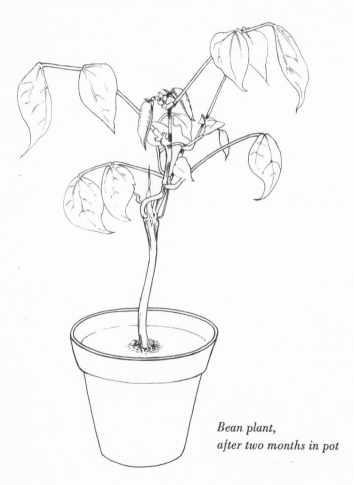

Bean plant,
after two months in pot

Within sixty days your plant may mature. At about that time, add a cupful of humus to the topsoil and gently turn it under.

After sixty days, a good healthy plant will produce charming bean blossoms, and, when they drop off, small beans will begin to develop. I once knew a professional bean farmer who told me that it is advisable to pick the first crop of beans when they are very small. Thereafter, all new beans are left to grow at their own rate of speed. It is believed that this practice prolongs the period of bean productivity; that is, the plants grow greater crops when the first beans are plucked. I cannot vouch for this system, because in our house the first, smallest beans are plucked and eaten on the spot before any plans can be made to set up a control for later productivity. Yet every once in a while we manage to resist random picking long enough to harvest a small crop of beans. Then we eat them fresh—they are delicious— and while doing so we drink fitting toasts to the fertility of the beautiful bean.

3
✿ sweet potatoes and yams ✿

The sweet potato plant has never quite made it into the parlor. Even in our palmiest days we have judged it as a peasant, a common garden-variety vegetable with easygoing manners that got it consigned to the confines of the kitchen. Where it flourished, it was usually in an old jelly glass filled with water, and since its rapid ready growth requires no special care or facilities, it was not much of a challenge to gardeners intent on adding rare and exotic plants to their indoor environments. But whether cultivated in the kitchen in a glass of water or advanced to a nobler role in a pot of good earth in the living room, a sweet-potato vine is a lovely and lavishly productive performer, willing to decorate any place it is put.

When the bottom of a sweet-potato tuber is kept wet in a container of water, it begins to root vigorously, and at the same time the upper section of the tuber begins to display outbursts of tiny purple-red leaf buds. These tightly curled leaves quickly unfold and develop in a variety of forms, colors, and textures. The early leafage changes from small heart shapes to three-inch broad and double-lobed leaves. Copper and alizarin leaf-edges turn pink and become light-green and then dark-green. The leaf's veins, outlined on a blue-green or fading pink ground, are distinct and boldly marked. The surfaces of the leaves are crinkled, crisp, and

24

shiny, as if freshly waxed and burnished, or they are smooth and flat with a matte finish. The leaves are supported on strong short stems, which are attached to radiating vines that are tough and stubborn, yet curiously pliant, and often jointed with elbows to accommodate shifts in direction. The over-all effect is a curling, twisting, expansive, generously leafed vine that twines clockwise while climbing across and over itself in a greedy quest for light and living space.

It is not possible to predict the way any given potted yam or sweet potato may develop. Happily, the differences in plant sizes, shapes, life spans, and life styles are more or less predictable. Depending on the size of the tuber, the life span of any given plant varies from six months to two years. Some sweet potatoes are climbers, others are crawlers.

Sweet potatoes and yams are botanically separated into two distinct groups. The sweet potato is a member of the large *Convolvulus* family, which is composed of some four hundred species and countless varieties of tuberous plants, many of which are climbers and display big colorful blossoms such as the morning glory. The yam is also a member of a large family, *Dioscoreaceae,* genus *dioscorea.* This group contains some two hundred and fifty species and hundreds of varieties that, like the sweet potato, are cultivated in practically every tropical and semitropical climate. For a reader unfamiliar with the tubers, sweet potatoes are mostly long in shape, yet sometimes rounded. They measure from three to eight inches long and from two to three inches in width. Their pale yellow skin is roughly textured, and the flesh, also pale yellow, is a bit dry and firm in texture. The sizes of yams are similar to those of the sweet potato, but the skin of the yam, also rough, is orange-colored like the flesh, which is generally soft and moist, except in larger specimens, where the flesh is inclined to stringiness. For retail distribution both sweet potatoes and yams are often artificially colored bright orange. Both vegetables are often subjected by commercial growers to a process known as kiln-drying to inhibit sprouting in transit and in storage. Because the process does in fact discourage growth, I always buy sweet potatoes and yams in shops specializing in organically grown vegetables, since they do indeed root far more readily.

Several varieties of yams and sweet potatoes are available in the marketplace. However, in most food markets there are usually no marked differences between the tubers, and only an expert could differentiate between the varieties.

Even in these inflationary times, a yam or a sweet potato still remains an inexpensive item.

༄ PLANTING

MATERIALS NEEDED:
A whole sound sweet potato or yam
A glass large enough to fit the tuber
Toothpicks to support the tuber in the glass

༄ *Rooting the Tuber in Water*

The bottom end of the tuber (opposite the stem end) is usually the broader end, but this is not always so and it is not always easy to tell which end is down, especially when the tuber is a round one. However, don't worry. Upside down or right side up, in soil or water, a fertile sweet potato will find a way to accommodate its eagerness to root.

Be sure to choose a sound tuber, that is, one without mold or soft spots. Cut off one-half inch of flesh from one end, and about halfway up from that cut, firmly push in some toothpicks in a circle around the tuber. Using the tooth-

Sweet potato, after two weeks in glass

26

picks as support, balance your sweet potato across a glass filled with enough tepid water to keep the tuber's bottom awash. This water should be kept at a constant level. Now place the glass in a warm, darkly shaded spot, and keep it there, checking the water level occasionally, until roots appear.

The roots are variably formed: some grow long, thin, and in dense tendrils; others grow only one or two long, thick, ropy strands. In expectation of either kind your glass should be large enough to give room for a free, full fall of roots. A darkly colored glass may be used, but a colorless glass vessel makes it easier to note the development of roots, which is an enjoyable sight.

Your tuber may not take root at once. Some take longer than others to get started. The time can be as brief as ten days or as long as six weeks. Don't give up on it. When a tuber is not fertile and fails to take root, the odor of decay will unmistakably inform you of that condition. Dump the tuber and start over again. On the other hand, once the roots begin to fall—and tiny red leaves will appear even before roots are well established—it is time to pot your sweet potato to insure a longer-lasting plant.

Sweet potato, after four weeks in glass

Sweet potato,
after six weeks in glass jar

Transplanting into Soil

MATERIALS NEEDED:

Two terra-cotta pots, one a six-incher, the other
an eight-incher (make certain that the pots
have adequate drainage holes, whatever size
you decide to use, and that they are generously
crocked)

Crocking materials

Dish to go under pot to catch water overflow

Humus-enriched, sterilized soil

Plant food

The size of the pot depends on the size of the tuber. A six-inch pot is the right size for a four-inch tuber, but if the tuber is fatter than three inches across its middle, you had better use an eight-inch pot. I generally avoid planting long skinny sweet potatoes. I know this is a prejudice, based on my feeling that a long skinny tuber might produce a long skinny plant—which is not necessarily so. At the same time, it is true that the larger the tuber, the longer-lasting the plant.

After crocking your pot, fill it with soil to within two inches of its top. Put the pot in a plate to catch the water overflow, and water-soak the soil. Then, from the center of the pot, scoop out a hole deep enough to accommodate as many of the roots as possible, leaving all the buds exposed to air. Pour water from glass into soil, and add more soil to within one inch of the pot's top. Firmly pat the soil down around the tuber. If necessary, add more water so that the soil is well soaked. Place the pot in sun or artificial light. From here on guard against scorching or freezing weather.

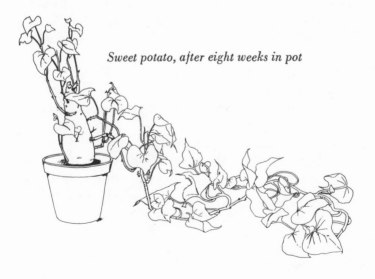

Sweet potato, after eight weeks in pot

Sweet potatoes and yams are prone to attack by mealy bugs. (For control of that infestation see page 59 on "Planting Practices.") Mealy bugs proliferate in a hot, dry atmosphere. Therefore, it is advisable to mist-spray regularly, at least once a day. Every other week or so, whether bugs appear or not, mist-spray all parts of the plant with a mixture of mild soap (such as Ivory), and tepid water which you have worked up into a good head of bland bubbles. *Do not use detergents of any kind.*

When a leafed vine appears and starts reaching outward, you may now begin to give the plant as much light as possible. If the only available light is artificial, provide at least five hours a day under two 100-watt incandescent bulbs. Four weeks after potting, give plant food, and repeat at four-week intervals. And consider the direction your variously winding vines begin to take.

Left to its own devices, the plant may be a climber or a creeper. Whatever its inclinations, however, turn the potted plant around in the light so that all sides are equally well lit. Soon the vines will spread out over every surface in view. On reaching the end of a flat surface they will fall and grow downward. It will seem that an exploratory tendril is always reaching for something to latch onto. At this point, you can cut back on some vines or you can construct a trellis to support the plant's climbing ambitions. It's all a matter of personal preferences and interior décor. In our house, I recently placed a life-sized sculptured head in the center of a low round table, about thirty inches in diameter, which had been overtaken by the dense lush foliage growing from three potted sweet-potato plants. The head, a reproduction in dark stone, is a strong, demanding statement and I was able to coax several vines to grow around its base. Then I moved the table into full sunlight. In no time at all, the fresh new leafage beginning to grow across the sculptured face needed to be thinned out and cleared away. Every day thereafter it became necessary to redirect new sets of climbing greenery. In the meantime, however, the searching foliage continued to complement enhance, and soften the sculpture's stony presence. And now, between the stone sculpture and the reaching vines, a live, green, symbiotic relationship has been handsomely established.

4
🙖 elephant's-ears, OR TARO 🙔

I know of no other indoor plant that grows with such swift generosity as elephant's-ears. Cultivated in a good-sized pot, a moderately large taro tuber may germinate within two weeks after planting and continue to put forth foliage for another eight months thereafter. And what a production it is!

When the first shoots emerge they rapidly rise to become firm, fat stems heavy with moisture and tightly curled leaves. In graceful arcs, the stems grow up to thirty-six inches tall, and as the great leaves unfurl they seem determined to grab all the warmth they can get from the sun or the nearest light bulb. Taro leaves are elegantly heart-shaped, velvety in texture, blue-green in color; they measure up to eighteen inches from their pointed tips to their curved ends and as much as twelve inches across their middle. The outer edge of each delicately veined leaf is finished with a slightly raised border, one-quarter inch wide, which looks like an invisibly stitched hem.

The plant is a veritable reservoir of water. As each new leaf opens and develops, its tip and edges are embellished with small, evenly spaced drops of clear water. Should an unwary admirer get in too close for a better look, the suspended globules fall in a shower both delicious and refreshing.

Best known to us by its descriptive name, elephant's-ears, *Caladium colocasia* is a member of the Arum family, which includes the lotus, jack-in-the-pulpit, calla lily, and philodendron. Said to be indigenous to the East Indies, the plant can now be found in most parts of the tropical and semitropical world, where it has long been valued for its nourishing edible tuber and large succulent leaves. In Hawaii, Tahiti, and Samoa the tubers are first boiled, then pounded and kneaded until reduced to the famous sticky paste known as *poi*. In the West Indies, where the tubers are called eddo, baddo, and coco, the huge leaves enjoy the charming name callaloo. In Southern sections of the United States taro is described as a bog dweller, and is also called dasheen. In Latin American countries the plant is found in a variety called malanga, which is the vernacular for taro flourishing in that neck of the woods. Where it is also grown and dubbed yautia blanca.

Taro tubers are available in sizes from three to six inches long, and from two to three inches in circumference. The skin is brown-black in color; its texture is rough and slightly hairy; and its flesh is so white that when exposed it seems to glow. In another variety, also small, the skin may be dark yellow, and the flesh lighter yellow and more porous than the white-skinned type. Whatever the variety, the tubers are club-shaped objects with blunt ends. The five-inch taro tubers can cost as little as fifty cents for a package of two.

✿ SOURCES

In neighborhood supermarkets I have bought taro packaged as *yautia blanca,* and in Spanish bodegas I have found the tubers labeled simply taro. I have also seen taro packaged as malanga in slices obviously cut from a much larger species, which is said to measure up to six feet and weigh up to a hundred pounds.

Sliced taro is fine for cooking, but since one does better

starting with an undamaged seed for planting, I always buy taro tubers intact and of a size to fit an indoor potting. (Besides, in view of the fertility and speed with which elephant's-ears grow, I am a shade nervous about the possibility of becoming involved with an enormous variety that somehow might manage to germinate despite being sliced, and could grow monstrous enough to crowd my household outdoors.)

Although I've never cooked a taro tuber or eaten any of its parts, I am told that fried taro chips and thoroughly cooked taro leaves, are simply delicious. It must be noted, however, that all parts of the tuber and its leaves have a distinctly acrid flavor, which is due to the presence of calcium oxalate crystals in the plant's cells. Careful preparation and cooking neutralizes the chemical and removes the bitterness. But I would certainly hesitate before eating any part of the taro plant raw, or cooked by anyone inexperienced in its preparation.

✣ PLANTING

MATERIALS NEEDED:

A pot, or pots (for a four-inch tuber use an eight-inch pot, at least; for a five-inch tuber, get a pot of at least ten inches)

Humus-enriched sterilized soil

Crocking materials

Plate to catch water overflow

Plant food

Because it is sensible to plant a tuber bottom end down, the question of which end is down is a matter of interest. In some varieties a smooth, brown, leathery patch develops at the bottom, and in other varieties annular rings of growth develop at the top. But this may not always be so. Therefore, when the markings are unclear, I judge the

34

bottom of a taro tuber by the direction taken by the fibers on the tuber's overcoat, which looks as if it had been curried with a brush firmly stroked downward. But do not worry. As with the yam, the position in which the taro tuber is planted is not all that critical to its future. A taro tuber planted bottom end up will germinate, and will most assuredly find a way to send shoots to the surface.

Potting

After making certain that the size of the pot matches the tuber's needs, fill the pot with humus-enriched sterilized soil to within two inches of the top. Place a dish for water overflow under the pot, and water-soak the soil, using tepid water. From the soil scoop out a hole deep enough and wide enough to accommodate your tuber comfortably. And leaving about one inch of the tuber's top exposed to the light, plant the tuber in the soil. Place pot in direct sunlight or in artificial light. After two to six weeks in the soil, the first signs of growth will appear. Interestingly

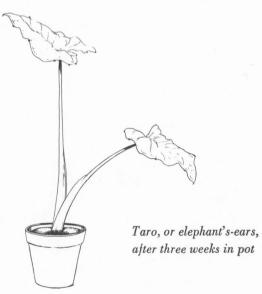

Taro, or elephant's-ears,
after three weeks in pot

35

enough, and possibly because of the way the tuber has been planted, the first shoots may occasionally emerge a good distance away from the tuber's tip. Or they may issue directly from the tuber's exposed top. When that occurs, the taro tuber looks like the head of a young goat, shaggy, rough, and complete with tiny, sharply pointed horns jutting upward and sideways. It's a pretty sight.

At this stage of its development, remove the plant from summer light, which may scorch the tender buds. Then, when the first leaves have unfurled, give it all the light available. If summer sunlight is not available, give artificial light from two ordinary light bulbs, 100 watts each, or from one reflector bulb, for four to six hours at a time. If sunlight is available but in poor supply, supplement it with artificial light two to four hours at a time.

Three weeks after the plant is in leafage, I add two plant tablets to the soil and plentiful measures of tepid water. If you are using a different variety of plant food, double the usual dose. Watch out for cold drafts and protect the plant against temperatures below 38° F. Then stand back and marvel over the swift development of your lovely elephant's-ears.

Taro tubers are great gifts to bring to city friends with indoor, outdoor, or no gardens at all. Started in the spring outdoors on an apartment terrace, or grown indoors in winter, in a window box or pots, taros combine most handsomely with other quick-growing tropical plants.

For example, just as soon as I finish writing this section I am going to prepare and plant a recently acquired redwood box. It measures forty inches long, twelve inches wide, and twelve inches high. Each end of the box will be planted with a fat yam or two, and alongside the yams I'll try a ginger or two. And alongside the ginger, and taking up most of the box's central space, I'm going to plant six taro tubers with their tips in the air. One of these days the arrangement should make a beautiful showing. And after watching the leaves reach for the sunlight in their various ways, there will come a time for cutting back and returning the leftovers to the soil. Then the box or parts of it will be ready for yet another planting, another recycling.

Taro, after eight weeks in box

5
✿ GINGER ✿

The ginger's family name, *Zingiberaceae,* looks and sounds fittingly spicy for that wonderfully scented plant. And the plant *Zingiber officinale*—the variety widely cultivated for culinary uses—looks as if it were intended to cast a cooling shade on a condiment long held in hot and high esteem. The early Greeks and Romans prized the pungent flavor of ginger, and it is still favored in Oriental and Near Eastern cooking.

I started my first ginger plant indoors because it looked as if its root needed a chance underground. The plant did nicely, but only after I discovered that its root did not want a full underground planting. This is because a gingerroot is a rhizome, which is a rootlike stem that lies in an oblique or horizontal position above the ground or only slightly underground. Naturally following the path of the root, the sprouts appear in successive rows and develop into stems that put forth translucent, smooth, long, narrow, and fragrant light-green leaves. The leaves emerge from sheaths that appear in alternating shoots from the stem, which, indoors, grows to a height of fourteen to sixteen inches. In nature, ginger stems grow five to six feet high.

In our house we grow ginger not only for the leaves but also to savor the foliage, stem, and leaf. We are also given to plucking a fresh tender leaf or two to chomp on,

*Indian stone bowl
containing dried ginger leaf*

and to rubbing (with a bit of both leaf and stem) the inside surface of a bowl that will soon accommodate a green salad. The thin film of volatile ginger oil spread on the bowl's surface gives a subtle and delicious accent to the salad's makings. The indoor plant will produce leaves and stems for as long as a year following the first sproutings, which will occur within four to six weeks after positioning the root.

SOURCES

Back at the beginning of the spice trade, the price of ginger was prohibitively high and only a very few could afford it. These days, packaged gingerroots, once found only in shops that specialized in Far and Near Eastern foods and spices, may be bought in supermarkets. In one such market I recently bought a neatly packaged box that contained two gingerroots, each about five inches long, at a cost of thirty-four cents—a nice buy.

Gingerroots, knobbed and gnarled and rosy-tan in color, are available in sizes from three to five inches long—which is just about right for indoor plantings. Sometimes the roots are white-washed and look like poor pallid things (I haven't been able to find out why this is done), and I generally avoid these. Most roots have small knobs which are easy to twist off and away from the large body of the root. Occasionally I have twisted off one or two knobs and planted them, but nothing came of that, so I always plant the whole root.

39

PLANTING

MATERIALS NEEDED:

A gingerroot or two

Flowerpots, six or eight inchers, depending on size
of root

Soil in a mixture of three fourths general potting
mixture, to one fourth sand, both sterilized

Crocking materials

Dish to catch water overflow under pot

Plant food

A six-inch pot will do for a five-inch root nicely, and a smaller root will need a smaller pot. I prefer to start with five-inch roots and six-inch pots. Cover the pot's drainage hole with at least two inches of crocking material. (Gingerroots do not thrive in a wet environment.) Fill the pot with enough soil mixture that the pot is filled to within two inches of the top. Thoroughly wet down the soil and smooth it to an even level. Next take up the gingerroot and after rinsing it in cool water—do not scrub—place the root across the moist soil, leaving some clearance between ends of root and sides of pot. Remember to press the root gently downward, held and placed in a horizontal position. The objective is to get no more than one quarter inch of soil across the root, which measures, usually, no more than one inch high.

Ginger,
after three weeks in pot

40

Place the potted ginger in a warm, dimly lit spot; water it with tepid water, but avoid soaking the soil or leaving water in the dish underneath the pot. When the first shoots show up, place the plant in direct sunlight and add plant food. During the summer months do not give more than an hour or two of direct sunlight. You can also put the plant in a situation where it will receive artificial light from two ordinary 100-watt bulbs for about three hours daily. Wash or mist-spray the leaves often.

The long graceful leaves that will appear on the stalk are sheathed. Sometimes they do not open, but simply stay put. Leave those mavericks to their own devices (most of them will dry out) but do not pluck them loose. Instead, allow the leaf to grow golden yellow. Then cut it loose and, using a small vessel—I use a tiny Indian stone pot with a tight lid—put snippets of the dried leaf in the pot for sniffing when you are so inclined. The odor is like that of newmown hay, with an overtone of a zestier scent.

It is said that ginger plants sometimes flower, and when they do it is on a shorter stem grown for just that purpose. Blossoms develop, like pine cones, in a dense cluster; they are sessiles, which means that they have no distinct support, but simply grow out from the main stem on their own.

Indian friends tell me it is believed that no mortal eye has ever seen the ginger plant bear fruit. But with such wondrous roots, leaves, stems, and scent, who needs fruit?

Ginger, after five weeks in pot

6
❦ pineapple ❧

On his second voyage to the Americas, Columbus revisited an island in the Lesser Antilles and while there noticed the natives eating a small, juicy fruit he had never seen before. Because it resembled a pine cone, Columbus named it the pineapple, and, preparing to sail north, he scooped up a few handfuls of the fresh new fruit, took them on shipboard, and sailed forth again.

Whenever I read anything about tropical or subtropical vegetation of the Americas, I find Columbus described as a generous distributor of largesse such as pineapples, guavas, sapodillos, passion fruit, and other exotica which he is said to have strewn across the face of both the Old and New Worlds. Perhaps that's how and when the pineapple became a symbol of hospitality in so many far-flung places. Whatever the story, here's to Columbus for carrying the fragrant, elegantly shaped, delicious, and beautiful pineapple to our shores. (Which is not to scant the missionaries who, at a later date, are supposed to have brought the pineapple to the Hawaiian Islands.)

The pineapple, *Ananas comosus*, belongs to the family *Bromeliaceae*, and it is a xerophyte (a plant especially adapted to survive long periods of drought).

The fruit develops from a dense cluster of small lavender flowers held upright in a nest of leaves, called a rosette.

Supported on a single stem, which may grow as tall as two feet, the flowers combine with their bracts to become fleshy and eventually the fruit itself is formed. Meanwhile, from the top of the developing fruit, there begins to rise yet another characteristic crown of leaves. In the mature plant, this crown produces leaves which grow in a series of out-ward-reaching arcs, and these in turn are followed by younger leaves growing straight up. The leaves are narrow, stiff, prickly-edged, slightly serrated, vertically ridged, sharply pointed at the tips, and half-folded inward. Pine-apple leaves are so cleverly designed that they act as half-shaded funnels to accommodate moisture collected from the atmosphere: each leaf is an efficient sluice for carrying all condensation and rainfall straight down to the heart of the plant. Moreover, each leaf contains specialized tissues for storing water.

Today, commercially grown pineapples are started from ratoons—which is a classy word for the suckers or offshoots that emerge from the base of the plant. The contemporary fruit is much larger than anything Columbus laid eyes on. The fruit takes about six months to ripen and mature, and seeds are only occasionally formed. Established plants bear fruit within one to two years in the fields.

SOURCES

Some indoor growers prefer to start pineapples in the spring. I think the preference is a leftover from a time when, in our northern markets, fresh pineapples were only available from March through June. These days the fruit can be found throughout the year in all manner of markets, not just the gourmet shops. Depending on the size of the fruit you may pay under a dollar for a small pineapple or up to two dollars for a larger one, though prices are too uncertain to quote them with any degree of confidence.

Every once in a while in the marketplace a pineapple shows up with green leaves striped white or yellow. Or occasionally one can find a fruit striped red on green. Most of the time pineapples have green leaves with a touch of silver, and finding them with different-colored leaves is a rather rare occurrence; such a fruit, when it appears, should be snatched up for instant eating and planting. (Among the bromeliads, which are decorative plants cultivated as such and not for pineapple fruiting, differences in colored leaves are a commonplace.)

It is impossible to claim that pineapple plants grown indoors are much of a horticultural achievement. They root easily and grow rapidly. All one needs is a good ripe fresh pineapple. As to judging ripeness, opinions vary, and systems are many. Floridians seem to swear by the ease with which a leaf is plucked loose from the crown. Hawaiians, on the other hand, prefer to snap a finger against the side of the pineapple, and, looking knowledgeable, declare that one responsive resonance means ripeness while another means the fruit is not quite at the peak. I judge a pineapple's ripeness by its softness and distinctive odor. Good and soft means good and ripe, and the unmistakable fragrance accompanying that condition also means that I've got a golden-ripe pineapple in hand. If the only fruit available is green and definitely unripe, it can be bought and brought home to stand in the fullest sunlight or in artificial light until ripe. Green pineapples tend to soften slowly and patience is needed, but keep a close watch on the ripening process. Once started it can be surprisingly swift. An unripe pineapple will not take root and grow.

 PLANTING

 *Rooting in Sand*

MATERIALS NEEDED:

A good ripe pineapple

A Pyrex glass pie plate, of a shape and depth used for baking deep-dish pies, at least three inches

high and six inches in diameter (you can substitute any other vessel of the same size)
Coarse sterilized sand, enough to fill the plate
three-quarters full
Plant food

Hold the pineapple firmly against a tabletop. With
a sharp knife cut off from the pineapple's top a two-inch
chunk of flesh along with the crown of leaves. This leaves
you holding the two-inch slab of flesh and the crown of
leaves in one hand, and the rest of the pineapple on the
tabletop. (Later you can skin the fruit and either eat it on
the spot or put it away for sharing with the family.)

Now put the truncated piece on its side, in a dish, where
it can be left exposed until a slight crust has formed over
the fruit's surface. This should take about twelve hours.
Then the crown of leaves and crusted flesh are ready for
placement in sand.

Fill your Pyrex dish with sand up to within half an inch
of the plate's top. Water the sand slowly, using only tepid
water, until the sand is no more than merely damp. Then,
gently but firmly, press the pineapple flesh into the sand
until the flesh is deep enough to keep the plantlet upright,
keeping at least an inch of sand between its bottom and
the bottom of the dish. Put two plant tablets into the sand.
Remove the planted dish into a warm, dimly lit spot, out of
direct sunlight. (I like to put the plate with pineapple
crown at the bottom of a closet.) Stand by for developments.

The plantlet should be left in the same dark, warm, and
sheltered place for as long as six or seven weeks, but no
more. During that period be sure to keep the sand constantly moist. After three weeks give plant food equivalent
to one plant tablet, and begin to keep an eye out for roots.
These may develop within the first two weeks, but because
a pineapple's roots are so short and fine—they are as white

45

Pineapple,
after three months in pot

and fine as dandelion down—it may be difficult to see them. So, gently lifting the plantlet at its edges, peer underneath for signs of tendrils. Replace the plantlet carefully. What is significant here is not the quantity of roots but the pleasant possibility that they have emerged at all. After two weeks in the plate of sand the fruit emits the lovely fragrance of ripening pineapple. By the seventh week it is quite likely that whenever the closet door is opened, the odor that drifts forth will have distinctly alcoholic overtones. However, as long as the crown of leaves remains green and fresh, all is going well. Keep looking for rooting, and be patient—sometimes roots are not easy to identify. If after seven weeks you cannot find roots, but the leaves are still fresh and the flesh smells good, get ready to transplant within the next day or so.

MATERIALS NEEDED:

A good-sized pot (anything under ten inches will not provide as generous leafing as a ten- or twelve-inch pot will)

Crocking materials

Humus-enriched soil and coarse sterilized sand, mixed three-quarters soil to one-quarter sand

Plate to put under pot to catch water overflow

Plant food

Mix the soil well. Crock the pot up to two inches and fill with soil to within three inches of the top. Water the soil until damp. Now bring the dish of sand and plantlet to the pot. Tenderly lift the crown of leaves and place it on the surface of the soil. Do not press into place. Instead, cover up the flesh of the fruit to the base of the leafed crown, securing the plantlet in place. Tips of leaves so dry and brittle as to be unbearably messy may be trimmed, but do not clip the leaves too far, or too many of them. Eventually they will fall free—those that are old and dry—to subside into the soil and nourish it.

Place the potted pineapple in shaded sunlight. Apply water but never so freely that soil is soaked. After three or four weeks move the pot into direct sunlight. The soil may be allowed to go quite dry, and it may be left in that condition for thirty-six hours at a stretch. Always use tepid water, and keep plant in a location where temperatures do not fall much below 45° F. Water directly into the center of the freshly emerging leaves. Water-spray the plant very sparingly—mostly to clean the leaves of dust. If sunlight is unavailable, substitute three to four hours daily of artificial light from two 100-watt light bulbs. Every six weeks add plant food.

It is said that flowering is encouraged by spraying the

center of the growing leafage with a mixture of plant food and water. Make the solution a weak one and let it stand for twenty-four hours. Then thoroughly rinse the leaves clean and also wash out the plate where water overflow may have gathered. Repeat every two or three months. I cannot vouch for this recipe because I have only tried it recently for the first time on a plant two years old. But who knows? Maybe it will work.

Should your plant produce a flower that turns into a full-fledged pineapple, tiny as it may be, here is yet another occasion for ceremonial eating and solemn celebration. And to mark the lovely pineapple's fertility, plant the fresh youngster in a plate of sand . . . and start all over again.

Pineapple,
after six months in pot

7
vegetable
tops

Some time ago it was believed that a good way to initiate a small child into the pleasures of indoor gardening, especially a city child unfamiliar with plant growth, was to assign her or him the simple task of planting and cultivating a vegetable top. Carrots, beets, turnips, rutabagas, radishes, and parsnips were considered suitable—though short-lived—plantlets for beginners. (That was way back when one could go into a vegetable market, ask for a rutabaga, and get more than a blank stare. For blank starers, a rutabaga is a variety of turnip.) Nowadays, young indoor gardeners are not discouraged even from the cultivation of "difficult" plants, nor from long-lived ones either, which is the way it should be, but nevertheless these are still charming plants and all respond to replanting.

SOURCES

Fresh vegetables bought in a supermarket—even when trimmed and plastic-wrapped—will sprout and grow. However, it must be said that the root vegetables bought in shops that distribute "organic" foods will start growing a bit sooner and may last longer than vegetables bought in the supermarket. True, the organic vegetables cost more than supermarket vegetables, but they often taste better, and in these days of inflated prices, it is impossible to evaluate

49

the "best" buy. But a "best" buy for planting purposes means that any of these root vegetables should be large in size and firm in texture.

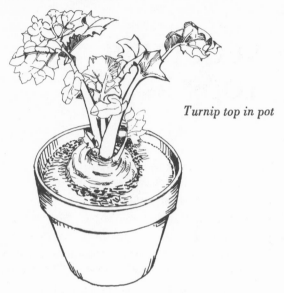

Turnip top in pot

PLANTING

MATERIALS NEEDED:

A good-sized root vegetable, carrot, turnip, parsnip, rutabaga, or beet (a carrot, for example, should be broad at the base and at least five inches long or longer)

A four-inch terra-cotta pot or a shallow dish five or six inches in diameter and three inches in height

A dish to catch water overflow

Coarse sand and humus-enriched soil, both sterilized, mixed half and half, and in a quantity to fill whatever vessel is used to within an inch of its top

Cutting horizontally, slice off two inches of the flesh from the vegetable top. Then fill the pot or dish with the sand-and-soil mixture, and wet it down. Next, stabilize your lopsided vegetable top until it stands upright. Add plant food equivalent to two plant tablets. Set the dish or pot out of direct sunlight, but not in the dark. Keep the sand-and-soil mixture constantly damp.

New sprouts will appear within two or three days after planting, and may continue for as long as a month. The leafage of each root top is different from others: carrots and rutabagas tend to grow curly tops; radishes, turnips, and parsnips tend to be more straightforward.

A NOTE ON FRESH BEET TOPS

Wondering if I could grow edible beet "greens," I once planted ten medium-sized beet tops in a Pyrex glass plate twelve inches in diameter and filled with half soil and half coarse sand. After ten days in its constantly wet medium, my still life put forth a delightful small harvest of fresh reddish-green leaves. Which I picked, rinsed, cooked a few minutes in lightly salted water, and then ate as a delicious tidbit for lunch.

GROWING A CARROT AS A PLANTER

Both junior and senior members of a contemporary indoor gardening family might consider the possibilities offered by a bright carrot. The whole vegetable can be scooped out and transformed into a self-planter, and left-over scraps can be eaten.

Choose a good-sized fat carrot. In one even slice, cut off an inch of the carrot's top. The objective here is to scoop out the carrot's innards and still have a leak-proof shell. The job is a bit of an engineering feat, but I use an apple corer and work with patience and caution. You may end up with more carrots for dinner than you bargained for, but it's worth trying. The outcome is charming.

51

When the carrot is freed of enough internal pulp that it can accommodate a tablespoon or two of water, stop excavating. Take up a needle and thread it with at least eighteen inches of stout thread. About an inch and a half below the top of the opened carrot, push the needle through the flesh, from one top end to the other. Evenly match up ends of thread, cut the needle free, and tie the thread in a firm knot at topmost ends. Fill carrot with water. If it leaks, try with another carrot. When everything is finally intact, hang this contrivance against a window pane, but not in direct sunlight or during a season when icy cold may freeze the carrot and hold it fast to the glass. If it is wintertime, place a piece of white paper over the glass and secure it firmly with Scotch tape. Fill the carrot with water and keep it filled at all times. Within ten days feathery, light greenery should have covered the outer surface of your bright carrot planting (it may take longer). This is a pleasing conceit to hang on the window of a room where a convalescent child, still in bed but well enough to have participated in the makings, can watch daily developments

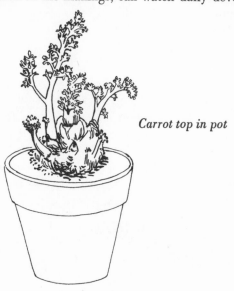

Carrot top in pot

A PUMPKIN IN THE OFFING

With another Thanksgiving season on the way, I plan on planting a pumpkin. I am going to buy and bring home a pumpkin of modest proportions and sound of body. First of all, the fruit will have to be washed with clear cool water. Then I will slice off the stem and enough flesh to get a space measuring eight to ten inches in diameter. After scooping and clearing out all the fruit's pulp and seeds, the festive vessel will be filled, one-third full, with a mixture of two parts humus-enriched soil to one part coarse sand, into which I will transplant a sweet potato previously and abundantly rooted in water. And because I have never before used a pumpkin in such fashion, after sparsely watering the soil, around the sweet potato I will plant a circle of pumpkin seeds—with thanks to the noble fruit and with hopes of growing a pumpkin vine to join the sweet potato. Vines within vines. There is a question whether the fruit will hold out and continue to function as a planter, so, as protection, and in the belief that the pumpkin can be secured as a vessel, I am going to apply a coat of liquid paraffin to the inside and outside surfaces of the shell before planting (see page 62 in Chapter 8).

BAMBOO POTS

Another lively vessel to consider: In the West Indies when a fat chunk of freshly cut bamboo arrives on a household scene, several sections, each two or three inches long, are cut off the larger piece. The short pieces are then filled with earth, planted with small seeds—such as morning glory—and should the bamboo begin sprouting before the planted seeds, which often happens, all to the good.

8
⠦⠦ General planting practices ⠦⠦

⠦⠦ POTS AND PLATES

Almost as old as the hills, terra-cotta pots probably originated in Italy (in Italian, terra-cotta means baked earth). By now there must be trillions of these pots everywhere, and each day more and more are being manufactured. Each terra-cotta pot is fashioned in fine, unglazed baked clay, so that the outer surface of the handsome, functional pot "sweats" when it is filled with earth. Each terra-cotta pot is also supplied with a drainage hole in its bottom. These properties are helpful assets for a plant trying to survive in an overheated home, especially in winter when our indoors can turn as dry as dust.

Terra-cotta pots are usually tapered from narrow bottoms to wider tops. Standard sizes range from two-inchers to twenty-four-inchers, or larger. The size is determined by measuring across the pot's open top and from top to bottom. For example: a four-inch pot will measure four inches across its open top, and four inches from top to bottom. Occasionally terra-cotta pots can be found in different shapes. Some may be tall and narrow—rare finds these days—others, more common, are half as tall as they are broad; these are called bulb pans and are designed for growing bulbs, of course.

Every flower shop, gardening-supply store, and five-and-ten carries supplies of terra-cotta pots. And despite rising costs across the land, these pots are still good buys.

✬❦ *Plates to Catch Water Overflow*
Terra-cotta plates are available for this purpose. But, like the pots, they sweat. This is not desirable for an indoor plant which is likely to be placed on a surface that may water-stain. I prefer Pyrex pie plates for catching water overflows. Pyrex plates come in many sizes, are easy to clean, can be found in any household-supply shop, and are reasonably priced. Besides, the glass nicely complements the terra-cotta pots, and does nicely for plastic pots, too.

✬❦ *Plastic Pots*
Although I don't like plastic pots, it must be said that they are lightweight, inexpensive, and when they are supplied with drainage holes can be useful. However, do not acquire or use a so-called self-watering plastic pot. This contraption is molded in one solid hunk of plastic, and has several holes punched through the plastic in a circle just above the place where the pot is joined to the plate. In the course of time, growing roots escape the holes, start to grow outward—looking dry and dreadful—and the dish has to be filled so high that it overflows at the lightest touch. Soon the roots clog all the holes, and both you and your plant are in trouble.

✬❦ *Decorator Pots*
Most "decorator" pots lack drainage holes, and their use for the plants described in this book is questionable. However, should you own a handsome pot and wish to use it, put a terra-cotta pot of a slightly smaller size and shape into the decorator, providing an air space between the two. Across the bottom of the decorator pot, pile up a few stones or rocks—not so small so they get massed into a plug over the drainage hole; this will hold the terra-cotta

pot out of reach of the standing water that will inevitably collect into a pool at the bottom of the decorator.

✦ *How to Crock a Pot*

Most plants need pots with holes in their bottoms, but those holes must be crocked to prevent the roots from becoming waterlogged. The best and most convenient source of crocking materials is an expendable terra-cotta pot, smashed into two-inch-square chunks. To keep earthenware splinters from scattering far and wide, wrap a four-inch pot in several thicknesses of newspaper, and then with a hammer bang away. Be sure the pieces don't get smashed too small. What you want is a pile of crockery, preferably curved, which can be arranged across the bottom of the whole pot. Let the pile come to a heap directly over the drainage hole. Never use small pebbles or sand, or gravel; these materials tend to settle and obstruct the hole, and, once packed down, there goes your drainage system—gone to pot.

✦ CARE OF PLANTS

✦ *Watering*

Get in the habit of watering your plants at the same time of day. But never water or mist-spray when plants are standing in sunlight or under artificial light—it causes burning of leaves and leaf tips. Always use tepid water. When a plant becomes truly dried out, first water the top soil enough to cover it, then fill the plate underneath the pot and stand by. Capillary action will carry the water up to the plant. If necessary, repeat watering until plant is as wet as it needs to be.

A nicety—mostly enjoyed by big-city indoor gardeners— is the use of "cured" water. Curing is accomplished by storing water in an open vessel for twelve or more hours

56

before giving it to the plant. During that period chlorine gas will be dissipated, and the water becomes a shade purer. This is not vital to the plant, but the idea rather pleases me.

৵ঔৎ Mist-Spraying

Dry hot air is the curse of all houseplant culture. What is needed is a refreshment of the plant's leafage applied every other day, especially in winter or during dry spells of spring or in hot summer weather. For this purpose, one can use a bottle of the sort once filled with window-cleaning fluid. (Thoroughly clean the bottle before filling it with tepid water.) Or you can buy a mist-spray bottle in a gardening supply shop. However—it bears repeating—do *not* mist-spray when plant is in full light.

৵ঔৎ Light

Guard against summer sunlight when it is at its hottest—that is, when the plant is unshaded. Even for plants that are tropical by nature, such heating can have scorching consequences. Winter sunlight, especially in our temperate climate, is much more benign and can be given freely to most established plants. When using artificial light, always keep the plant at least ten inches away from incandescent bulbs or fluorescent tubes. Turn the plants about in their light so they do not grow one-sided. Guard against icy drafts and sudden drops in temperature.

৵ঔৎ Plant Food

Plant-food mixtures are legion. If you have a favorite it would be better to stick with it and try to resist switching from one to another. I like the small green compressed tablets that can be pushed into the soil when the time is ripe. And that time should not be oftener than every two or three weeks. Follow instructions on the label of whatever plant food you favor.

༄༅ Repotting

At regular intervals check your plants for pot size. If a plant has grown too large, the time has come to move it into a larger pot. Repotting needs to be handled gently. Carefully loosen soil around the perimeter of the pot, then try to shake plant loose. If there is enough resistance to require forceful tugging, better put the pot on a piece of newspaper and smash the pot to release that plant. Should the plant have become rootbound and the roots show signs of mold or rot, cut back the rotten roots with scissors. Do not worry about cutting back quite ruthlessly. Prepare a larger, crocked pot with additional soil, and transplant, offering the plant a new terrain of fresh, rich soil to grow in.

It is easy to determine the size of the pot for the size of the plant. When a plant is too large or too small for its pot it just looks wrong. It is a simple matter of proportion, which can be readily adjusted by transplanting.

༄༅ Mulching

In outdoor gardens cultivated in temperate zones, when the trunk of a tall tree does not provide shade for the ground beneath and around it, natural mulching helps to keep the soil cool during baking hot weather, and warm during freezing cold weather. In summer the earth surrounding the tree is protected and kept cool by green growing plants, grasses, and weeds, which provide natural ground cover. In winter the tree sheds leaves, and some shed fruit and nuts as well, and these, combined with summer dried grasses, provide winter mulching.

To bring the subject closer to home, when the leaves of a tall tree, grown indoors, fall on the earth occupied by that tree, one should allow those leaves to stay where they are to help keep down the evaporation rate in that soil. And then, because indoor gardeners can choose seasonal environments at demand, you can mulch at will.

58

ᴥᴥ *Insect Pests*

The scourge of gardeners everywhere, insect pests can be controlled by the use of insecticides. However, though the dangers of insecticides have been widely publicized, I must repeat that great care should be taken when using *any* insect spray indoors. This is not a matter to be taken lightly. Ventilation should be provided for the sprayee, and aerosol cans should be avoided.

The best way—theoretically—to maintain an insect-free indoor garden is to work with scrupulously clean plants, pots, soils, and accessory materials in a clean environment. Pots—new or old—should be scrubbed with hot soapy water before using, as should the plates for catching water overflow and the crocking materials. Plants brought in from the outside should be closely and suspiciously examined for signs of insect pests before the newcomers are allowed to join your indoor garden. Despite all precautions, every once in a while—and for often mystifying reasons—an insect infestation will occur. When this happens both pot and plant should be completely isolated for treatment. Then, when freed of pests, it may be allowed to rejoin its healthy companions.

The most commonly seen pests in indoor gardens are aphids, mealy bugs, red-spider mites, and scale. The first three are very small and it requires a sharp eye to spot them. The simplest way to deal with them is to spray the plant thoroughly with a mixture of half soap flakes and half tepid water, shaken until flakes are dissolved. Or spray with the stronger mixture of half rubbing alcohol and clean tepid water. *Do not use detergents.* Make sure to spray all parts of the plants as well as their pots and dishes for water overflow. Spray no more than once a day for as many days as are needed to clean up these destructive intruders. Once it is freed of pests, mist-spray the plant with clear water.

Black flies sometimes start buzzing around the base of a

plant, usually after food in the soil. A simple spray with water and a dash of dissolved soap will wipe them out.

The most devastating of all insect infestations to be seen in an indoor garden is scale. These are oval-shaped animal organisms. Adults are one eighth of an inch long; males are brownish, females whitish. These small monsters lie flat wherever they can get a purchase on the plant. They look as if they were covered with a heavy carapace—like that of an armadillo—and the weight of the carapace has squooshed them down. Small plants may be treated for scale by the use of a cotton swab dipped in rubbing alcohol, and then applied to scrub each insect into oblivion. But it is an onerous task. Scale is nasty, spreads rapidly, and the organism is very tough. If it succeeds in overtaking a plant, it is far better to dump that plant than risk infecting the rest of your garden.

Happily, these days there are natural insecticides that can be safely used indoors. I recently bought a product, packaged in a jar, that is a combination of cedar and hemlock oils, petroleum distillates, and soap. Mixed with water in my own spray bottle, this brew wiped out an infestation of mealy bugs. And it promises to be as effective with other insect pests that can plague houseplants. Called Ced-O-Flora, it can be found, priced inexpensively, in many of the new plant shops that seem to have sprung up. Follow instructions for this and any other natural insecticide—and always spray with windows wide open.

Another school of insect control is a preventive one. It advocates the planting of onions, shallots, or scallions with a foliage plant. But since an onion or any of its cousins needs its own ground, it is not always possible to spare the room. (A sweet potato overpowered by an onion is not a pretty sight.)

Then there are the champions of salamanders and praying mantises as agents for the control of insect pests. If I were to acquire one of these attractive little scavengers I am not at all certain what would need to be done should one of them wander off. So, until I read up on the needs and habits of these charming creatures, I will make do with what's at hand.

৯৯৩৪ Sand

City dwellers sometimes find it difficult to locate sand. On occasion I've swiped bagfuls from building sites, and I've been known to swipe bagfuls from beach sites. Taken from such sources, sand used for plantings needs to be sterilized before using. And that's easy enough to do— simply boil it for about ten minutes. Use only coarse sand of a variety called "builder's sand," which can be purchased in gardening supply shops. To repeat: it is important to use *only coarse sand*. Very fine sand is useless. It tends to pack down, or simply flow away, like water.

৯৯৩৪ Soil Composition

However mightily an indoor gardener may yearn for constant sources of soil supply, a city apartment seldom offers enough room to accommodate a barrel of loam or to ventilate conveniently a seething compost heap or a crate of decomposing leaves, all elements needed for good rich soil.

So we buy packaged soil. It's always a good idea to buy from dependable gardening-supply stores, five-and ten-cent stores, or anywhere else where the *packaged* soils are guaranteed sterile and where information on the labels will tell you what kinds of plants can be grown from the given mixture. In the case of packaged soils, a label should also inform you as to the ingredients in the package.

For example, a package of so-called "general" potting mixture is likely to contain loam, sand, leaf mold (which by another name is humus), bone meal, peat moss, organic fertilizers, etc., in correctly balanced proportions. Loam is a basic soil, a natural mixture of sand, silt, and clay. It is said that silt—a word probably derived from salt—is loose sedimentary stuff largely composed of mineral particles and clay. Clay is an earthy substance, made up of several kinds of decomposed rocks.

Another package may announce itself as being humus-enriched, which simply means that, added to the general potting mixture, a quantity of humus and charcoal has darkened the soil and also given it greater porosity. This is a desirable texture for houseplants. It is always important to use only sterilized soils. Unsterilized soil may contain microscopic insect larvae waiting for a chance to grow up and start eating indoor plants.

✖❧ *A Note on Soil*

When a plant is housed in a pot too large for it, the plant cannot use all the soil, and the roots cannot develop fast enough to handle all the water needed to keep the soil damp. As a result the soil's nutrients are dissolved or flushed away and the roots—slight as they may be—may also become waterlogged.

In the case of a plant that is too large for a pot, the nutrients in that soil will soon be used up and in an effort to make up for insufficient soil, the chemicals in the plant foods that may be given can go into solution and the plant's roots become "burned."

After a while, and following repeated watering, the top-soil of a plant becomes packed down. Loosen that soil. And use a fork, or any tool with blunt, short tines, to turn over the soil, gently, to a depth of about two inches. To avoid snagging the roots, work very carefully.

And now that the soil is aerated, smoothed, and softened, it's a good time to plant a patch of ground cover.

✖❧ *Mending with Paraffin*

Paraffin is the stuff used for sealing jars and glasses of homemade jellies and preserves. It is usually packaged in flat cakes, is available at most markets and hardware stores, and is inexpensive.

Nothing beats paraffin when it comes to restoring pottery, porcelain, and glass vessels with hairline cracks. This restoration is not likely to withstand pressure or heat, but for indoor gardeners with vessels that need repairs so they can be adapted to small plantings, paraffin is useful indeed.

For instance, a hairline crack I once found on the bottom of a large fish tank responded to a paraffin repair, even though its future role was limited. The tank then became a sometime terrarium that I used for starting cuttings and small-sized citrus seedlings, as well as a good number of bean plants. Another example: I repaired an antique Wedgwood eggcup that had a large crack from top to bottom. Now it supports a reasonable amount of water and a sprig of *Zebrina pendula* that overflows the cup with leaves and stems reaching in every direction. The cup has also supported dyed Easter eggs, carefully cracked open at the narrow top, emptied of their contents, and filled with soil scattered with a pinch of fine lawn grass, which has presented us with many a miniature spring lawn.

The material itself is very easy to apply. Simply heat a cake of paraffin in a metal pot over a low flame until the cake becomes liquid. To repair a crack across the bottom of a bowl, pour enough liquid paraffin into the area in want of sealing and slosh it back and forth until the crack is well covered from end to end. When the liquid has hardened, use cool water to test for leaks. If water placed inside the restored vessel seeps, apply another coat of liquid paraffin, and if need be another, third, coat of the liquid seal. For surfaces difficult to get at, use a small paintbrush dipped into the liquid paraffin and apply generously.

In the case of my pumpkin, after sloshing the liquid around the inner surface of the fruit, I will paint several paraffin coats on the pumpkin's outer surface before I begin planting.

❧ afterword ☙

Trying to figure out where I stand on the question of singing to plants for their welfare and improved development, I must say that I do not believe in it as a sure-fire method. On the other hand, I do think that indoor plants can become as neurotic as animals kept in zoos. But I can't quite come to grips with that unless I'm willing to see a relationship between animals and vegetable life, which is not easy either. Nevertheless, if singing to one's indoor plants makes the gardener feel better, I say sing away. My trouble is I have a singing voice that croaks, and I don't care to risk sending my garden into a depression. So, for now, I advise everyone to keep careful watch and to give close, habitual, and full care and attention to their indoor gardens; that way lies the sure development of a good green thumb. And while I tend my indoor plants and recognize my relationship with their development, I think I'll start practicing dulcet tones in which to murmur loving tributes to nature, who is the most generous and beautiful gardener of us all.